one throw at a time

HOW WE REDISCOVER CONNECTION THROUGH PLAY

DR. MICHELLE HASTIE THOMPSON

one throw at a time

HOW WE REDISCOVER CONNECTION THROUGH PLAY

DR. MICHELLE HASTIE THOMPSON

One Throw at a Time: How We Rediscover Connection through Play

Published by Absolute Love Publishing
USA

United States of America

ISBN: 979-8-9855746-5-4

By Dr. Michelle Hastie Thompson
The Weight Loss Shift
The Chakra Secret
Have Your Cake and Be Happy, Too
One Throw at a Time

Dedication

I dedicate this book to my son, Rome. Watching Rome thrive through connection reminds me of what really matters in life. He keeps me grounded, makes me laugh, and fills my life with absolute joy. I wouldn't be where I am today without his presence. May children continue to be our best teachers.

Contents

Foreword

I've spent a huge chunk of my life standing 27 feet away from a wooden board, competing and throwing cornhole bags for hours. To most people, cornhole is just a backyard pastime for tailgates and BBQs. But as a professional player for the American Cornhole League and three-time World Champion, I've seen the high-stakes, televised side of this game. I've felt the adrenaline of the last bag, the weight of the trophy in my hand, and the crushing weight of a big loss. Yet, if you asked me what keeps me coming back, it isn't the trophies. It's the people.

I met Michelle right as cornhole was exploding into a professional league. In the new world of sponsorships and stats, she showed up not just as a player or fan, but as someone fascinated by the "why" behind the throw. As a mental coach, she wasn't just looking at the physics of a throw; she was looking at the mental side of the players. Michelle immersed herself into the cornhole world through her multiple podcasts, commentating nationally broadcast games, and player coaching. Her passion and curiosity as to "why cornhole" was obvious to all in the cornhole world.

Our connection was instant because we spoke the same language: respect. I've always believed that sportsmanship comes first. You can have the perfect flat-bag, but if you don't respect the person across from you, you've already lost. She saw that in me, and I saw in her a deep understanding of why that connection matters. She knew that when we step onto the court, we aren't just competing—we're connecting. But she also understood the battle happening inside the player. In cornhole, your biggest opponent isn't the person on the other side of the board; it's the voice in your own head. True mental toughness isn't about being a robot; it's about having the resilience to stay present when the pressure is mounting and the bags aren't falling. She taught me that mental strength and player respect are actually two sides of the same coin. When you have the internal stability to stay calm and give yourself grace, you naturally have more to give to the community around you.

I've had a front-row seat to her magic during the women's cornhole retreats we host together annually. I've watched her sit with women who felt they'd lost their confidence or mental toughness both in their cornhole game and their personal lives. I have watched her explain the literal toll that staying connected and present in the moment takes on our bodies—how being disconnected isn't just a "bummer," it's a physical toll on our bodies. And the best part? I watched her use cornhole as the medicine. She showed us that "play" isn't a distraction from life's problems; it's the way we solve them. In the simple act of tossing a bag and cheering for a teammate, I saw lives change in real-time. I have witnessed Michelle rebuilding these women's confidence through the game, sometimes through something as simple as helping them feel confident in their shot selection. I saw the "rebuilding" process she writes about so beautifully in these pages. I have witnessed the connections she forms with each woman, and I have the honor of having my own connection with Michelle and being able to call her a trusted friend and valued colleague.

People always ask me what it takes to be a champion. They expect me to talk about practice hours or grip techniques. But the truth is, you can't be great in a vacuum. You need a community to hold you up. Michelle has been the champion and pioneer for emphasizing the mental aspects and personal connections in our sport, proving that our legacy isn't just our win-loss record—it's how we treat ourselves and other people along the way.

- Rosie Streker,
Three-time American Cornhole League World Champion

Introduction

When the phone call ended, I had no idea if I'd ever see my husband again. It was November 8th, 2018.

This was not the first tragic situation we had faced together. We wonder even now if we were meant to be together to face all the traumatic situations the world can throw at two people. But this story will begin on the day of the fire.

I remember waking up in the middle of the night with a gut feeling that something was off. It was unseasonably hot, even for California. It was incredibly windy, which is what woke me up in the first place. But even with that gut feeling, I never imagined I'd be part of the Camp Fire, the deadliest wildfire in California history.

Eighty-five civilians died as the fire swept through 153,336 acres, traveling the length of 80 football fields per minute and destroying 18,804 structures. In 2018, the town of Paradise had a population of about 27,000. By 2019, fewer than 5,000 people remained.

I escaped that morning with my young son and our dogs.

My husband barely made it out alive. My in-laws sheltered in a building that later burned to the ground. By nightfall, the only thing left of our home was smoke and memory.

In the days that followed, survival was the only focus: food, clothes, somewhere to sleep. We crammed into relatives' homes with nothing but mattresses on the floor.

The silence of losing our old way of life was deafening. Paradise was not just a place. It was neighbors pulling into our driveway because the garage door was open. It was nights in the backyard playing cornhole, cracking open beers, and laughing until it got too dark to see. What I missed most was not the things. It was belonging. Overnight, all of that was gone.

This was not my first experience with disconnection, but it was the most profound. It forced me to ask a question I had been circling for years: What happens to us when the places we belong disappear?

We shrink. We get sick. We lose hope. The answer is life-altering. Without connection, humans wither. With it, we thrive.

This book is about connection, why we need it, how easily we lose it, and how we can rebuild it in the unlikeliest places. For me, that doorway came through a simple game of cornhole. What started as a backyard distraction became a lifeline, then a community, and eventually a lens that showed me something bigger: Connection is not optional. It is essential.

Cornhole is my story's setting because it is the game that saved me, but this book is not about cornhole alone. It is about what happens when people come together around anything – games, groups, families, or neighborhoods – and rediscover themselves in the process.

You will notice three layers woven together as you read. My story shows the experiences of fire, loss, rebuilding, and finding a new community. I've also included evidence-based material, with research on belonging, motivation, and social connectedness that explains why connection so deeply matters. Finally, there is practice that shows how to bring connection into your life and the spaces you influence. I call the framework HUMAN™.

Connection cures. It heals isolation, softens trauma, expands possibilities, and builds resilience. It is not a luxury. It is as vital as food, water, and rest. I hope you walk away from this book not only convinced of the power of connection but also equipped to bring it into your own family, workplace, classroom, or community.

When the fire stripped everything away, I thought I had lost my future. What I found instead was that connection can be rebuilt, one conversation at a time, one gathering at a time, one game at a time.

That is the invitation of this book, to remember what we already know in our bones: that we belong to one another. And when we choose to connect, we change not just our own lives, but the lives of everyone around us.

Part I:

The Quiet Loss of Connection

The Anatomy of Disconnection

Disconnection is rarely sudden. It slips in quietly, often unnoticed until its effects are undeniable. At first, it might look like busyness, the gradual crowding out of friendships by work schedules, deadlines, and family obligations. It might look like scrolling late into the night, convincing ourselves we are too tired to make a phone call or invite a friend to dinner. It can creep into marriages where partners live parallel lives, into workplaces where colleagues sit side by side but never truly know one another, and into families where everyone is in the same room, separately.

The body often feels disconnection before the mind can name it. Research shows loneliness increases stress hormones, raises blood pressure, and weakens immune function (Holt-Lunstad et al., 2015; Seppala, 2023). Over time, the toll is profound. Social isolation has been compared to smoking 15 cigarettes a day, with risks greater than obesity or physical inactivity (U.S. Department of Health and Human Services, 2023). It shortens lives, not by months, but by years. Loneliness is not just unpleasant. It is lethal.

And yet, when people talk about disconnection, they rarely use clinical terms. They talk about feeling out of place, about not belonging anywhere. They describe walking into a room full of people and feeling invisible. They talk about the silence after a loss, the empty calendar on a Friday night, or the ache of knowing that even the people closest to them do not truly see them. Disconnection convinces us not just that we are alone, but that we are the kind of person who does not belong.

I know that ache personally. In middle school, I felt it every single day. I was not an athlete. I was not part of the popular crowd. I did not even feel at home in my own skin. I hated my hair, my face, my body, and I longed to disappear. I believed I had only two choices. I could blend in by becoming just like the people around me, or I could risk being invisible. I chose the first path.

I tried desperately to be with the cool kids. I laughed at their jokes, agreed with everything they said, and tried to dress like them. Sometimes it worked. I was invited to parties or allowed to sit at the lunch table. But I never felt like I belonged. I felt lucky to be there, like I had snuck into a place I was not supposed to be. Every invitation felt fragile, as if the slightest misstep would expose me as an outsider again. What I did not understand then was that this was not belonging. It was desperation. It was the exhausting work of performing in hopes that acceptance might follow.

Looking back now, I see I was not simply insecure or trying to fit in. I was disconnected. I had no place where I felt at ease, no space where I could show up without effort and know that I was welcome. That absence of belonging shaped how I saw myself for years.

That same ache returned decades later, though in a very different form. After the fire destroyed our home in Paradise, California, I was not just grieving walls and belongings. I was grieving the rhythm of life that had made me feel grounded. I was grieving backyard nights with neighbors, the comfort of knowing someone would drop by unannounced, the simple security of being known.

In the months after, we had a roof over our heads, but I felt hollow. Every day carried the weight of what was gone. The silence was deafening. It was the absence of connection, and it was every bit as destabilizing as the loss of our house. What surprised me was that grief was not just about the physical losses. It was about the loss of people, routines, and community. It was about feeling unmoored in a world that no longer resembled the one I had built my life around.

This is what research now helps me understand. Disconnection is not a weakness. It is not laziness. It is not proof that something is broken inside us. It is a signal, one as biological as hunger or thirst, telling us that something essential is missing. Psychologists Richard Ryan and Edward Deci refer to it as relatedness, one of three universal psychological needs outlined in Self-Determination Theory (Ryan & Deci, 2000). Without relatedness, without belonging, we do not simply feel lonely. We function less effectively in every domain of life.

And yet, the cultural messages we receive rarely tell us this. Instead, we are told to hustle harder, to achieve more, to numb our ache with work, money, or accomplishments. But the evidence points in the opposite direction. The antidote to disconnection is not independence. It is not climbing higher or running faster. It is connection. And connection does more than soothe. It strengthens resilience, lowers stress, protects against disease, and restores joy (Holt-Lunstad, 2021). Connection is not a luxury. It is medicine.

I first noticed this truth years earlier when I worked with women in the weight-loss industry. Again and again, I saw their lives held no room for play. They were devoted to their families, diligent at work, but when I asked what they did just for themselves, I was met with silence. They had no outlets for joy, no close friendships outside of obligation, no spaces where they could show up and simply belong. Without play, their focus narrowed until it landed entirely on the scale. Their bodies became the only arena they felt they could control, and that hyperfocus left them lonelier and more disconnected than ever.

One woman told me she had not gone out with friends in years because she was embarrassed about her body. Her evenings consisted of work, dinner for her kids, and television until bed. Another admitted she did not have anyone she could call if she wanted to share good news. These women were not lacking willpower, motivation, or discipline, as they so often believed. They were lacking connection. They had structured their lives around responsibility and achievement, but the absence of play had left them with no outlet for joy and no place to belong.

I gave my clients assignments to increase their connection to their bodies and themselves. But I didn't have a solution to connect them with a network in their community quickly. I didn't have a hack to help them instantly find their people and fulfill their need for relatedness. I would tell them to make a list of things they could do in their spare time. Many of them laughed, "What spare time?" while others couldn't fathom what to do with that time. I spared them lectures about how humans will always make time for what's important to them. I knew we weren't dealing with logic in those moments. Emotions were in charge, and I needed a creative solution for connection that wouldn't raise the typical resistance barrier most exercises do when it comes to asking a human to change. It wasn't until years later that I found it.

Disconnection has patterns, and once you know them, you start seeing them everywhere. It thrives in the small gaps we dismiss as usual: the friend we mean to text back and forgot, the neighbor whose name we still don't know after years on the same street, the dinner table where everyone scrolls through separate screens. None of these moments are catastrophic, yet together they drain the system that keeps us human.

I began to notice these micro-separations in daily life. In public spaces, people wore earbuds instead of exchanging glances. In workplaces, meetings ran efficiently but rarely warmly. Even within families, everyone was "together" but oriented toward different glowing rectangles. The form of connection was still present; the substance had thinned. It was like breathing air with less oxygen. Technically enough to survive, but not enough to thrive.

What made this realization more unsettling was how socially accepted disconnection had become. We celebrate self-sufficiency, idolize busyness, and equate solitude with strength. The person who needs nothing from anyone is often admired. Yet the very independence we praise can quietly turn to isolation. When the need for belonging is ignored, the mind compensates in predictable ways: overworking, overcontrolling, numbing, or attaching to anything that offers a brief illusion of being seen. The behaviors differ, but the motive underneath is the same – an attempt to feel safe in the absence of connection.

Research captures this drift in measurable ways. Time-use studies show that in the past two decades, Americans have lost nearly a full day each month of in-person social interaction. Loneliness has risen across every age group. But numbers only tell part of the story. The lived experience is far subtler. It is teachers who eat lunch alone because there is no time between classes, retirees who no longer receive phone calls from former coworkers, and parents who feel unseen in their own homes. Disconnection rarely looks dramatic. It looks like ordinary life missing its pulse.

One of the most deceptive qualities of disconnection is how reasonable it seems. We tell ourselves we're just tired, or focused, or that this is what adulthood feels like. We rationalize the absence of community as a matter of logistics, distance, cost, or schedules, without recognizing the physiological hunger beneath. In that sense, disconnection operates like dehydration. The longer it lasts, the less accurately we can register the need.

The body keeps signaling, though. It does so through irritability, fatigue, and the subtle dulling of pleasure. Neuroscientists describe loneliness as a state that sensitizes the brain to social threat. In isolation, we become more vigilant, scanning for cues of rejection. The brain's alarm system stays on. Over time, that constant activation fuels inflammation, sleep disruption, and hormonal imbalance. We call it burnout, but much of what we label as burnout is simply the body protesting prolonged disconnection.

What makes this pattern so hard to detect is that it can look like stability. From the outside, a disconnected life often appears orderly: work gets done, routines stay intact, responsibilities are met. But internally, something begins to dull. The days lose contrast. Moments blur together. Without the friction of shared life, conversations in passing, unplanned laughter, the energy of other people, experience flattens. Nothing is technically wrong, yet very little feels alive.

That is what disconnection does: It erases texture. It removes the small unpredictabilities that give life dimension. Conversation turns into an information exchange. Movement turns into transportation. Meals turn into refueling. Even joy becomes scheduled, managed, optimized. The very aliveness we crave can't survive under that kind of control.

When I finally studied the science behind it, this understanding started to click. The same stress pathways activated by physical danger are triggered by social isolation. Our species survived through cooperation; the body still remembers that. To feel cut off from others is, on a cellular level, to feel unsafe. No wonder people describe loneliness as heavy or cold. The nervous system is interpreting absence as a threat and signaling the body to brace.

What makes this epidemic so difficult to address is that it rarely announces itself. People don't go to the doctor and say, "I'm disconnected." They say they can't sleep, can't focus, can't stop scrolling. They say they're anxious or unmotivated. We treat the symptoms – insomnia, stress, depression – without tracing them back to their social roots. Disconnection hides inside diagnoses that sound more clinical but are often relational.

Understanding this changed how I see nearly all of life. It reframed my past experiences not as personal shortcomings but as natural responses to unmet needs. It also reshaped how I view our culture. We have built systems that reward isolation and then act surprised when people feel lonely. We design neighborhoods without sidewalks, jobs without community, and technologies that mimic intimacy while eroding it. Then we tell individuals to meditate, exercise, and take care of themselves on their way back to health, alone.

Recognizing the anatomy of disconnection doesn't solve it, but it gives it a name. And naming restores agency. When we can identify what is happening, we can stop personalizing it. We can see loneliness not as proof of inadequacy, but as evidence of our humanity doing precisely what it's designed to do ... signal that something essential is missing.

We don't always recognize ourselves in the word disconnected. It can feel too clinical, too dramatic. If that word doesn't quite land for you, try these quieter signals:

Do you ever feel surrounded by people but somehow separate from them?

Do you feel like you're always "on" but rarely *with*?

Do your days feel full but your heart feels a little empty?

Do you find yourself scrolling more than speaking, observing rather than engaging?

Do you want deeper relationships but feel unsure where they would even fit?

Maybe the loneliness doesn't show up as sadness. Maybe

it shows up as irritability. Or exhaustion. Or the urge to withdraw because connection feels like one more task on an endless list.

Perhaps you've caught yourself craving community while simultaneously dreading the effort it might take to get it. Or maybe you've quietly stopped reaching out because you don't want to be the only one trying. These are signals. Signals that you are human. Signals that you were built to belong. Signals that something in you is asking to be seen, supported, or simply *with*.

If you recognize even one of those internal whispers, then you belong in the pages ahead. You don't need to have a name for what you're feeling. You just need to be willing to notice it. Because what disconnection erodes, connection can restore, one small moment at a time.

Why Adults Stop Playing

By the time most of us reach adulthood, play has quietly slipped out of our lives. As children, it is unquestioned. We chase each other on playgrounds, invent games that spill across backyards, and enter imaginary worlds with the ease of breathing. Play is how we learn, how we test boundaries, how we make friends, and how we discover who we are. But somewhere along the way, the rules change. We are told to grow up, to be serious, to trade imagination for responsibility. Slowly, the space for play shrinks until one day we realize it is gone.

This loss is not just about fun. It is about connection. Play is one of the most natural ways humans bond. It lowers our guard, creates shared experiences, and provides a safe space for us to experiment with forming a sense of belonging. When play disappears, so does one of our easiest entry points into community. The result is a quiet loneliness that many adults carry without ever naming it.

As a mother, I have watched my son easily insert himself

into groups of kids he's never met through play. As a toddler, he would hop on the slide next to another child and then they'd run back up together to do it again. He'd find the train table at the bookstore, and he and another kid would hop into an imaginary world together. Now that he's older, much of his play includes electronics and gaming, but it still allows him to start a conversation with another child he's never met.

My childhood was full of forts, LEGO® sets, and playing house. My best friend and I spent entire afternoons building imaginary worlds, choreographing routines and performing skits for my parents who pretended not to know the ending. In high school, Mario Kart™ became the icebreaker; inviting someone over to play felt safer than asking, "Do you want to hang out?" We didn't call it connection then, but that's exactly what it was: shared focus, easy laughter, the comfort of side-by-side fun. Looking back, I can see that play was the language connection spoke before self-consciousness entered the room, before we believed belonging had to be earned.

Without shared interactions – those small, effortless touch points – being around people can start to feel awkward or even intimidating. Most adults don't want to walk up to a stranger and comment on the weather. Or even if we do, we don't know how to take the conversation to a place of more connection. We need a *reason* to begin, something that lowers the social stakes and gives us a shared focus. As kids, play created that focus automatically. As adults, we often lose the built-in activities that help conversations unfold without force. When there's no natural way in, avoidance becomes the easier option. So we keep ourselves busy instead. Checking tasks off the list, convincing ourselves productivity is a perfectly acceptable substitute for connection. It feels responsible, even admirable. But what it usually signals is that we're filling time with what's available rather than what we actually need.

In college, this became even clearer. I had finally reinvented myself at California State University in Long Beach. After years of wanting to disappear, I was now trying on a cloak of confidence, determined to be noticed. I took a job at the gym's kids' club just to get a free membership. On the day I went in to fill out my new-hire paperwork, the fitness manager asked me to walk the floor and talk to people. I did what came naturally. I listened. I came back with a stack of stories from members I had chatted with, and to my surprise, he hired me on the spot for a different position. Just like that, without certifications or experience, I was suddenly responsible for training adult clients.

At twenty-one years old, I leaned into it. Within months, I had a roster of clients and was teaching people how to move their bodies, chase their goals, and push through fear. From the outside, it looked like I had it all together. But inside, I was still hustling for worth. Training clients did not feel like play to me. It felt like survival. I was terrified of being exposed as someone who did not know enough, terrified of my body not measuring up to the image of a "real" trainer, terrified that if I stopped pushing, everything would fall apart. I had taken one of the most playful environments – the gym, a place built for energy and endorphins – and turned it into another arena to prove I was enough.

Most of us know this feeling. The place where we look confident but stay braced, expecting one misstep to expose us. Where we keep striving because slowing down feels dangerous. Where we're surrounded by people yet convinced we're one mistake away from being found out. We call it insecurity or imposter syndrome, but underneath those labels is something simpler: disconnection from our own humanity.

This is not unusual. Research shows that as children move into adolescence and adulthood, time spent in unstructured play drops dramatically, while time spent in achievement-focused activities rises (Lester & Russell, 2008). We are funneled into sports where performance is measured, into classrooms where grades are the currency, and into jobs where productivity is the metric of worth. The spontaneous joy of play is replaced by the pressure to perform. By adulthood, most of us do not stop playing because we no longer need it. We stop because we no longer permit ourselves to see its value.

If you pause and look back, you can probably trace your own drift. Maybe recess became practice. Maybe drawing became "not good enough". Maybe you traded bike rides for to-do lists, dance parties for deadlines, friendships for group chats. You didn't decide to abandon play. You simply learned which parts of yourself the world rewarded, and joy rarely made the shortlist.

And to be clear, we haven't stopped consuming entertainment. We binge shows, scroll endlessly, and chase digital dopamine through games and apps. But zoning out isn't the same as tuning in. Passive distraction doesn't restore us the way play does. Play asks something different … presence, silliness, creativity, a willingness to be seen without performing.

That was the part I had forgotten. I was good at being

efficient, at striving, at proving. I was less good at being alive. It took a moment that forced me to stop, quite literally stop, to realize how far I had drifted from myself.

That moment happened in 2008 when I was hit by five cars in a freeway accident. For years, I had been living in overdrive. I was obsessed with calories, exercise, and discipline, convinced that if I just pushed harder, I would finally feel good in my own skin. But after the accident, I was forced to stop. I could not train clients, I could not control my food intake, and I could barely stand on my own some days. What filled the gap was not more hustle, but connection. Friends drove me to appointments. My new boyfriend, Nick, cared for me. My body began to heal when I finally surrendered. I did not know it then, but surrender and play share a commonality. They both bring us back into connection, out of control, and back into relationship with ourselves and others.

What I have come to understand since is that adults rarely lose the *capacity* for play; we lose permission. Somewhere between adolescence and career, we internalize the belief that play is childish, that it signals laziness or lack of ambition. The word itself becomes embarrassing, something reserved for kids or retirees. We disguise it under more acceptable labels — hobby or self-care or recreation — but what we mean is the same thing: a state of doing something purely for the experience of doing it.

Play requires presence, and presence demands vulnerability. To play is to admit we care about something that might not matter to anyone else. It asks us to risk looking silly, to risk failing without consequence, to release control long enough to be surprised. Adults are not trained for that kind of openness. We build our days around what must get done, errands, carpools, deadlines, logistics, and then hope we have something left over at the end. Most nights, we don't. We collapse on the couch with nothing but the energy to scroll. The problem isn't that we don't want joy. It's that our lives are so tightly scheduled around responsibility that spontaneity doesn't stand a chance. The more overwhelmed we feel, the more we cling to structure, believing that control will calm us. But control doesn't calm; it contracts. It squeezes out the space where connection, curiosity, and the lightness of play once lived.

In the years after my accident, I started noticing how often adults confuse leisure with play. They sound similar, but they serve completely different purposes. Leisure is a break from effort, rest, recovery, relief. It's collapsing on the couch after a long day, scrolling TikTok, watching a show, taking a weekend trip where the goal is to do as little as possible. Leisure helps us refill the tank.

Play doesn't refill the tank, it changes the fuel.

Play is voluntary engagement that sparks energy instead of draining it. It's laughter that arrives before you realize you're laughing. It's losing track of time because you're so absorbed in the moment. It's movement or creativity that feels like freedom instead of obligation. You don't play to recover from life; you play to feel alive in it.

For a long time, my life was full of leisure but void of play. I could rest, but I couldn't access joy. When I asked friends what they did *just for fun*, there was always a pause, a blank look, a nervous laugh, a shrug. We could list our responsibilities instantly. But joy? We needed a minute. Some couldn't remember the last time they did something purely because it delighted them. Others insisted they didn't need fun, they needed productivity, which is what happens when disconnection convinces us that usefulness is the only form of worth.

Play used to be our default. Somewhere along the way, it became a luxury.

Researchers have observed what could be called a *play gap*, the steady decline of play from childhood into adulthood. In early grades, creativity and movement are abundant; by middle school, both decline sharply. By adulthood, the average person spends less than two percent of waking hours in any activity that could be described as playful. Studies show that adults who rate themselves as playful also report higher creativity, resilience, and social connection (Proyer et al., 2018). The capacity for play doesn't disappear; it just goes dormant under layers of obligation.

Play also suffers from inequality. Time, money, and safety all influence who gets to play. Parents, caregivers, and people working multiple jobs often lack the freedom for spontaneous fun. Gender expectations deepen that divide. Men are often encouraged, even celebrated, for spending time on hobbies like golf, fishing, or video games. Their leisure is viewed as a legitimate need, a way to unwind. Women, on the other hand, are expected to use their free time to support others or improve something: organize the house, catch up on errands, call a friend who needs advice. My clients could rationalize a workout because it burned calories or "earned" relaxation, but an hour of painting, dancing, or wandering? That felt indulgent, like it needed justification.

The absence of play changes more than mood; it changes physiology. Neuroscientist Jaak Panksepp identified play as one of the brain's core emotional systems, rooted in subcortical regions that also support joy, social bonding, and learning. When mammals are deprived of play, their social skills and adaptability deteriorate. Humans are no different. Chronic play deprivation narrows our emotional range and stiffens our thinking, long before it shows up in the body.

I can see that stiffness in old journal entries from my twenties. Every page is about goals – income goals, body goals, relationship goals – but there is no mention of joy. I mistook busyness for meaning. When I wasn't working, I was planning how to work better. I believed that structure equaled safety, and I was terrified of what might surface in stillness. What I didn't realize was that play is not the opposite of work; it is what makes work sustainable. It replenishes the curiosity that effort consumes.

When play disappears for too long, the future narrows. We stop imagining new possibilities and instead cling to what already feels predictable. We become efficient but uninspired, productive but disconnected from any sense of aliveness. Little frustrations start to feel like proof that life will always be this tight, this rushed, this serious. Without room for spontaneity, dreams get practical. Risks feel reckless. The parts of us that once believed in adventure quietly go dormant. We keep moving forward, but the life we're moving into feels smaller than the one we once pictured. Our days become something to manage rather than something to experience.

There were small glimpses even then. Cooking with music on instead of measuring every macro. Going to the beach without counting it as cardio. Laughing with my future husband Nick while playing games. These moments didn't register as productive, so they didn't seem necessary. But they were the only times my nervous system downshifted. I see now that they were tiny rehearsals for rediscovering play … unstructured, purposeless, human.

You might have glimpses like that, too. Moments that feel good for no reason. A long shower where the world finally quiets. A walk where you notice the sky instead of your steps. Singing along to a song you forgot you loved. And yet, if you're anything like me, those openings can get crowded out quickly. A podcast goes on in the shower so the time feels productive. A scroll fills the silence in the grocery line. A chore replaces the urge to sit down for a minute. We don't set out to avoid the downshift, we just forget that we need one.

Culturally, we tend to romanticize childhood play as a phase we outgrow rather than a skill we must preserve. But play is not an age; it is a mode of being. It is how the mind integrates emotion and experience, how relationships deepen without the pressure of purpose. Anthropologists have found evidence of adult play in every known society through music, dance, sports, and storytelling. What varies is not whether adults play but whether the culture permits it. In modern Western life, permission has eroded.

This loss matters because play is practice for connection. It teaches flexibility, empathy, and trust in safe, low-stakes settings. When adults stop playing, our tolerance for uncertainty shrinks. We become brittle in the face of difference, anxious when things don't go to plan, and overly attached to control. The consequences ripple far beyond leisure; they touch how we parent, lead, and relate. Without play, collaboration becomes performance, and curiosity becomes strategy.

Think about how easily play used to arise. A stick became a wand. A cardboard box became a spaceship. As adults, the same imagination could transform a dinner, a conversation, or a walk if we allowed it. But the imagination that once expanded the world now serves mainly to anticipate disaster. We have repurposed creativity for worry. Reclaiming play is not about doing less work; it's about remembering how to approach life with wonder instead of defense.

Play does not require equipment or extra time; it requires permission. It can live in how we talk, how we move, and how we notice. It's there when we let a song pull us into dancing while we cook or when we laugh mid-conversation instead of hurrying to make a point. These are not trivial gestures. They are nervous-system resets, small reminders that we are safe enough to let go.

I've learned that for many women, softness doesn't feel safe at first. We spend years in "high mode", managing households, careers, caregiving, crisis after crisis. Our nervous system adapts. Even when life calms down, our minds go searching for the next thing that might require vigilance. A quiet evening feels strange. A moment of stillness feels like we're failing at something. We tell ourselves we'll relax when everything is done, but everything is never done. Play becomes uncomfortable not because we don't want joy, but because our bodies have forgotten how to receive it.

When I look back on the times in my life when I felt most grounded, they all share one thing: unguarded engagement.

It didn't matter what I was doing … only that I wasn't performing. I've written songs to heal, and I've written songs trying to write a good song. The latter never works. The moment I start trying to make something impressive, the connection disappears. But when I create from honesty, something opens. That is the paradox of adulthood: everything we chase through effort already lives inside the ease we've forgotten how to access.

The disappearance of play isn't a moral failure; it's a social inheritance. We absorbed the belief that responsibility and play cannot coexist. But responsibility without play breeds rigidity, and rigidity kills connection. Understanding that pattern is the first step toward undoing it. Later, I would discover how easily play returns once the right conditions appear. But first, it had to be missed deeply enough to recognize what had been lost.

Fixing vs. Connecting

From 2009 to 2019, I spoke with thousands of women who wanted to lose weight. They came to me sure that if they could just master one more plan, one more rule, one more round of willpower, something would finally click. These were not women who lacked knowledge or discipline. Most of them already ate well and exercised regularly. They could list calories in an apple from memory and had gym bags packed by sunrise. Yet no matter how much effort they poured into their bodies, their sense of peace never arrived.

They were deeply invested in *managing* their bodies, but not in *listening* to them. The more they tried to fix themselves, the further they drifted from themselves. It wasn't laziness holding them back; it was disconnection.

I used to believe discipline was the highest virtue. It had certainly saved me in moments when my life felt chaotic. But I began to notice that discipline without relationship turns cruel. The women I worked with weren't thriving from structure; they were shrinking under it. They spoke to themselves like drill sergeants, berating, bargaining, withholding approval until the next weigh-in. It reminded me of a parent who hovers over a child with constant correction: The attention is intense, but the connection is absent. And like any child, the body eventually rebels.

When I asked these women simple questions, such as, "How does your body feel when it's tired?" or "What does hunger feel like for you?" many couldn't answer. They had outsourced every signal to an app or a scale. Their bodies were data points, not partners.

Over time, I realized they didn't need more information. They needed *permission to feel.* They needed curiosity instead of control. However, when they began to soften, to eat without punishment or move without tracking, the first thing that surfaced wasn't joy – it was emptiness. All the energy that had been tied up in control suddenly had nowhere to go.

That void terrified them.

To fill it, I encouraged them to experiment with things that had nothing to do with food: walking groups, book clubs, dance classes, pottery nights. Sometimes it worked. A few rediscovered the laughter they hadn't felt in years. But many came back discouraged. "It's not the same," they'd say. And they were right. What they wanted wasn't an activity; it was belonging.

When belonging is absent, the human mind scrambles for substitutes. We chase productivity, perfection, or constant self-improvement because they provide the illusion of progress. But progress is not connection. We can sculpt a perfect routine and still feel hollow.

There were women who admitted they'd reach their goal

weight, yet the victory lasted less than a week. They thought they would feel free, but instead, they were terrified of gaining it back. Fixing never ends. There is always something left to tighten, to track, to optimize. Connection, by contrast, asks nothing of us except that we show up as we are.

The myth of fixing runs deep in our culture. We are conditioned to believe that happiness is the reward for perfecting ourselves. If I had the body, the house, the partner, the savings, *then* I would relax! But the pursuit itself fractures us. We trade intimacy for image, presence for performance. We even bring the fixing reflex into our relationships, trying to solve people instead of sitting with them.

When I began studying psychology, I finally had language for what I had been witnessing. According to Self-Determination Theory, human beings have three core psychological needs:

Autonomy: the freedom to choose our actions from desire, not pressure.

Competence: the feeling that we can be effective in our lives.

Relatedness: the sense of belonging and being connected to others.

When those needs are met together, we feel grounded, motivated, and whole. But when even one is missing, the system wobbles.

The women I coached were hyper-focused on competence, doing it right, and proving they could, but what they were building competence in was being the best dieter. The person they wanted to become, someone who feels at home in their body, wasn't being practiced at all. Autonomy was sacrificed to rules. Relatedness faded as they isolated themselves from the world while waiting to become "acceptable". Competence without connection is brittle. It may produce results, but it cannot produce well-being.

Relationship Motivation Theory extends this idea further, suggesting that the quality of our motivation, whether it's controlled or connected, determines how sustainable our behavior is. When motivation is driven by guilt, fear, or pressure, we may comply, but we burn out. When it's fueled by belonging, we grow.

That is why no amount of "fixing" worked. They were trying to earn worth through control, when what the body, and the psyche, needed was safety. Safety can only emerge in connection.

We see the same dynamic everywhere self-improvement becomes the goal instead of the by-product. Wellness culture, for example, often sells connection through control: Track your macros, your steps, your mindfulness minutes. But what begins as care easily mutates into measurement. The more metrics we collect, the less we trust our own signals. The body stops being a home and becomes a project. The same pattern shows up in personal development. We call it growth, but much of it is performance. Chasing the next self-help book, the next breakthrough, the next optimized version of ourselves. None of it is wrong, but without connection, even healing turns into hustle.

In the years I coached, I watched entire industries monetize this hunger for improvement. It didn't matter whether it was business coaching, fitness, or mindset work, the message was the same: Do more, try harder, become better. But people weren't craving transformation; they were craving togetherness. What they wanted wasn't to be fixed; it was to be felt. To sit in a room where someone nodded and said, "Me too." That moment of resonance does more to change a person's life than any plan or protocol ever could.

Connection and fixing are incompatible states. Fixing invokes a hierarchy in which one person demands and another obeys. Connection elicits parity in that both people belong. Fixing requires certainty, while connection invites curiosity. When we fix, we try to earn belonging. When we connect, belonging is a given. Fixing turns life into a solo performance. Connection integrates by turning effort into collaboration, achievement into shared joy.

Outside of sports, the same principle applies. In workplaces, the fixing reflex appears as burnout. We call it high standards, but it's often loneliness in disguise. Employees chase metrics to feel valued. Leaders manage people like tasks. Entire teams lose sight of each other as human beings. In families, fixing shows up as constant correction, partners trying to improve one another, and parents trying to optimize children. We mistake control for care.

But connection requires a different posture. It's slower, softer, and far more vulnerable. It means listening before advising and being present before performing. It asks us to trade "How do I fix this?" for "How can I be with this?"

I learned this lesson the hard way. After the Camp Fire, when everything familiar was gone, I tried to rebuild my life like a project plan: a new house, a new schedule, and new goals. None of it made me feel better. The only thing that eased the ache was community, everything from friends who cooked dinner to strangers who donated clothes. Healing didn't happen because I rebuilt my life perfectly. It happened because people engaged with me when my life was messy.

The same is true at every level of our culture. We are living in an age of optimization. Our devices track sleep, steps, productivity, and even mood. Yet the more data we collect, the lonelier we become. We keep improving our systems while neglecting our souls. A 2023 Surgeon General's report on loneliness calls this the next great public health crisis. It warns that disconnection increases risk for heart disease, stroke, dementia, and depression. But statistics alone can't capture what that really means. It means millions of people moving through their days unseen. It means parents too tired to play, coworkers too busy to talk, and communities built around efficiency instead of empathy.

What I found through both my clients and my research is that belonging is not a by-product of success; it is the prerequisite for it. When we feel connected, our nervous system relaxes. The prefrontal cortex reengages. Creativity and motivation rise naturally. We stop grinding and start growing. That's the biology of connection; it literally reorganizes us from the inside out.

That is the invitation of this chapter: to recognize how often we try to repair our emptiness with strategy when what we need is belonging. The shift is subtle but profound. Fixing asks, "What's wrong with me?" Connection asks, "What's needed here?" Fixing strives to control. Connection chooses to relate. Fixing is fueled by fear. Connection is built on trust.

We cannot hustle our way into wholeness. We cannot punish or perfect our way into peace. But we can practice connection, in our bodies, in our families, in our communities, and watch how the need to fix begins to dissolve.

When we belong, the system recalibrates. The body softens. The nervous system steadies. The mind stops grasping for the next solution because, finally, it feels safe.

That is where healing begins, not in control, but in connection.

And that is where we turn next: What it actually means to practice connection, to build environments, habits, and communities that remind us daily that we are, and have always been, human.

Part II:

Finding Connection Where You Never Thought You Would

From Disconnection to the Boards

What surprised me most after the fire was how easily disconnection can hide inside a perfectly normal-looking life. On paper, we were fine … working, parenting, paying bills, making meals. From the outside, there was no emergency. Inside, there was erosion.

We drove to friends' homes when asked, but it now had to be planned. We had no neighbors where we could casually offer, "We're throwing dinner on, want to come by?" Without those unplanned touch points, days were scheduled rather than shared. What used to be community felt like an event to organize.

A neighborhood can be full of houses and still feel empty if the design discourages bump-into-you moments. Long commutes eat away at the margins where friendship often thrives. Busy roads without sidewalks make casual encounters rare. When the places people gather are expensive, noisy, or centered on buying rather than being, families quietly opt out. We say people are isolated, but often the environment creates the isolation. Walkable blocks, shaded parks, open community centers, and predictable weekly gatherings have the opposite effect. They make connection the default rather than the exception. Healthy communities aren't just individuals making good choices. They're places where good choices feel natural.

It helped to name a distinction I'd missed for years: Solitude isn't loneliness. I like being alone. Chosen quiet restores me. Loneliness sets in when quiet is no longer an option, when you want to be known but cannot find a way. You feel it on the couch at night or in a crowded room surrounded by conversations that exclude you. Presence without connection is its own kind of isolation. Naming that difference kept me from pretending I didn't need people. Connection doesn't erase solitude, but it does make solitude safe.

Disconnection rarely travels alone. It brings irritability, numbness, the sense that time is passing, and the feeling you're watching your own life from a few feet away. After the fire (and a later home invasion), my nervous system stayed on high alert. I wanted to relax in my own home, but the body keeps score and mine excelled.

Connection doesn't undo trauma, but it changes the conditions in which healing can happen. When trustworthy people are nearby, the body gradually stops bracing for impact. The heart rate settles. The breath deepens. You laugh without planning to. Belonging tells the nervous system the present is safe enough to feel. Seen through that lens, my research stopped feeling like statistics and began to feel like a map.

Earlier, I introduced the Self-Determination Theory, which encompasses autonomy, competence, and relatedness.

Those aren't abstractions – they show up in neighborhoods and households. Autonomy means having real choices about where to spend your time, rather than just reacting to urgency. Competence feels like being effective at something that matters. Relatedness is knowing where to go on a Tuesday night and who will be there when you arrive. Most of us aren't missing all three at once. We're usually low on one or two. In my hardest seasons, autonomy shrank to survival, and relatedness thinned to almost nothing. Competence stuck around because I know how to work. That combination made me look steady on the outside while feeling unsteady inside.

None of this means we wait for a perfect town or calendar before we try to connect. It means we're kinder about why it's hard. If your schedule leaves no margin, the connection will feel costly. If your neighborhood lacks places, connections will require planning. If your history taught your body to expect danger, connection will require courage. These are barriers, not verdicts. The goal isn't to shame ourselves for feeling disconnected. It's to find the smallest next move that makes belonging more likely.

So I tried small moves. I joined a mothers' group hoping for peers, but the conversation stayed surface-level. I took a dance class and even asked the instructor to hang out afterward, but she politely declined. I kept putting myself out there, doing all the "right" things, but nothing seemed to click. The effort felt forced, and the loneliness deepened because I was trying to make it work. The missing piece wasn't just meeting people; it was finding a container where connection could happen without performance.

That container turned out to be play.

Where It All Began

We had a version of cornhole in our backyard. My now-husband Nick had been playing in local cornhole tournaments for a while, and most weekends, I tagged along to watch. I stood behind the boards and studied the rhythm of the throws, the thud of bags on wood, the easy banter between people who clearly knew each other. From the outside, it was simple: two boards, a few bags, a lot of laughter, but something about it was magnetic. It made me curious. Why would a backyard game matter this much to grown adults?

I practiced in our yard for no reason beyond being with Nick. After dinner, we'd head outside with a drink and talk while we threw. At first, I was bad. Then I wasn't. Progress came quickly enough that one night Nick looked over and said, "You're ready."

I had stood in the tournament hall a handful of times as a spectator. Walking in as a player felt different. The room buzzed, every lane full, the thuds of bags almost like applause. I recognized faces but not names, and my hands trembled as I pulled out my bags. Many local tournaments pair partners randomly so I wouldn't even be with Nick. It was just me, a scoreboard, and a stranger.

My first opponent smiled, cracked a joke, and held out his fist for a bump. That small gesture was enough to ground me. I took a breath and released my first throw. Smooth. Clean. It landed and stayed. In that moment, I wasn't watching anymore. I was in it.

The night settled into a rhythm: throw, wait, throw, wait. Between turns, people discussed work, kids, or their favorite bags. The tone was competitive but kind, focused without fear. After rounders, the event shifted to bracket play, and someone cheered every time I hit the board. Late in the night, I made a rookie mistake, tossed a bag I shouldn't have even thrown, dropping my opponent's bags in and costing us the game. Embarrassment flashed, then faded. Instead of shame, I felt lit up. I couldn't wait to come back.

That night taught me something I didn't yet have language for: Belonging is felt before it's understood. It arrived in the fist bumps, the mid-game tips from strangers, the way people reset the scoreboard as if to say we always start fresh.

At first glance, cornhole doesn't look like something that could change a life. It isn't extreme or elite. But its simplicity is precisely what gives it power. The boards are always 27 feet apart. Everyone throws the same distance, plays by the same rules. That sameness levels the field. A retiree and a 20-year-old can compete side by side. A family of four can play together without special gear. There's no uniform to buy, no fitness requirement to meet. You just show up and throw.

The structure invites conversation. You stand beside your opponent, not across from them. The pace: throw ... wait ... leave room for talk. It might start with "Nice shot" or "What bags are those?" and move into where you're from and how long you've played. Through the cracks of competition, connection finds its way.

Cornhole culture is different in that the distance between pros and everybody else collapses. You can watch someone on a livestream on Saturday and then play against them locally the next week. That accessibility removes hierarchy and reminds everyone that no matter how skilled you are, you stand the same distance from the same hole as everyone else.

When I interviewed competitive players for my Ph.D. dissertation, I didn't know what I'd hear, but I recognized the terrain. Hearing their experiences was powerful. Again and again, a pattern emerged: a nervous arrival, an unexpected kindness, and a quiet sense of having found their people. A former college athlete described the pain of losing his team. He stumbled into cornhole for something to do and then found a new home of friends. Others talked about showing up alone and leaving connected. The uniting thread wasn't the score. It was the ritual of play.

Looking back, I can see how cornhole reflects the needs I named earlier. Those pillars of Self-Determination Theory – autonomy, competence, and relatedness – are quietly built in. It's the freedom to do something just because it's fun, the satisfaction of getting better, and the bond of doing it alongside others. Cornhole meets all three regardless of what a theory suggests.

It isn't therapy, but it heals. It isn't family, but it feels like one. It isn't community service, but it serves the community. It invites people to show up as they are and rewards them for doing so.

That first night changed more than my Friday plans. It cracked something open. I walked in unsure and walked out sure I'd found something worth keeping. I didn't yet know how deep it would go, but I knew one thing for sure: I would be back.

And I wasn't alone. Across the country, in garages, casinos, backyards, and barrooms, people were showing up for the same reason: to throw a few bags, shake a few hands, and remember how to belong.

My Cornhole Addiction

After that first tournament, I couldn't stay away. What began as a way to spend more time with my husband turned into something that quietly claimed every spare thought. If I wasn't throwing, I was replaying missed shots in my head or listening to cornhole podcasts. Nick called it practice. I called it therapy.

Our backyard became the heart of it. When Nick got home from work, we'd grab a drink and head outside. The light would fade, our son Rome would wander in to toss a few bags or call the score, and the thud of bags on wood became our evening soundtrack. Some nights we talked about everything: work, bills, weekend plans. Other nights, we barely spoke, the shared focus its own kind of conversation.

Those evenings were about more than improving a throw. They were how we stayed connected in a season of rebuilding. After years of constant motion, standing side by side felt like the first stillness we'd had in a long time. For an only child, those small celebrations mattered to Rome, too. Four in a row, a high-five, easy laughter. It was family time without forced effort. Just play.

But the closest tournaments were 40 minutes away. One night, I looked at Nick and said, "What if we start something here?" Within a month, we had a date, a venue, and, most importantly, support. The Friday-night club we'd been attending didn't just wish us luck, they loaded up their trucks, brought boards and score towers, and helped us run our first tournament. They also wanted a club in our town. There was no territorial vibe, no competition, just people making more room for play.

Because of their help, the first night was doable. About 60 people showed up, and you could feel it in the room: relief, excitement, and the sense that something new was brewing. Word spread quickly. We outgrew that first space and moved to the casino in town. Wednesday nights swelled into a weekly ritual.

At some point, it hit me: We hadn't just started a club; we'd built a community.

Watching that community take shape felt like seeing my efforts to understand my need for connection come alive in real time. Players who barely knew each other showed up early to set up boards. Families attended, and the kids ran around playing while their parents competed. People lingered after the tournament elimination to keep spending time together. I watched the first-timers walk through the door with the same nervous energy I'd felt. Each time, the room responded with warmth.

When I later analyzed my interviews with competitive players, three themes ran through the stories: belonging, emotional shift, and social connection.

Belonging showed up first. People described cornhole as an anchor: a steady, predictable space in a life that often wasn't. One person laughed that he could walk through a mall in another city and still run into someone from the cornhole world. A single parent told me when she moved to a new town, the local club became her family.

Then came the emotional thread. Everyone remembered the same beginning: nerves, self-doubt, shaky confidence. The ending, though, was joy. Whether they won or lost, the experience of being included changed them. For some, it quieted long-standing anxiety. For others, it rekindled a sense of purpose. One player told me that no matter how hard his week was, he could count on the constancy of the boards. "They're always 27 feet apart." That reliability was his reset button.

Finally, there was social connection. Couples played together. Parents and teens shared weekends at tournaments. Groups that met through the game started camping trips, poker nights, and fundraisers. Play spilled into real life.

Listening to these stories, I realized that the behavior changes professionals try to engineer were happening here organically. People showed up because they wanted to, not because they had to. The structure of the game met their needs.

Cornhole reintroduces what adult life often squeezes out. It's simple but not shallow. Structured but not stiff. Grown-up enough to feel legitimate but freeing enough to heal.

I noticed how often people came for one reason and found another. A man joined after divorce, hoping for distraction, and left with a circle of friends who helped him rebuild. A woman grieving a loss said the game gave her a reason to leave the house again and people who noticed when she didn't show up. A couple who'd never played sports together discovered competing together strengthened their marriage.

These weren't just nice stories. They were evidence of what happens when humans are given safe ways to reconnect. Even failure felt different here. Missing a shot didn't isolate; it invited encouragement. That's what belonging does, it turns failure from threat into invitation.

Week after week, I watched connection regulate people who didn't have clinical words for what they were experiencing. They called it a mental break or therapy or the only place they felt like themselves. The terms were casual; the effects were real.

What started in our backyard grew. Running tournaments led to deeper relationships, and soon I wasn't just organizing local events. I was helping shape conversations around the sport itself. I launched a cornhole podcast to bring more women into the sport. The show gained traction, and people across the country tuned in. That visibility caught the attention of the American Cornhole League. I was invited to commentate and then moved into on-air roles as a commentator and sideline reporter. One step at a time, I went from tossing bags in the yard to working inside the organization growing the sport.

Today, I know thousands of players worldwide. I've stood on national stages, interviewed champions, appeared on ESPN and CBS, and watched the game transform lives in real-time. Through it all, my message has stayed the same: Connection cures. A casual hobby became a career, and more than that, a mission to show how play brings us back to ourselves and to each other.

I call this chapter "My Cornhole Addiction" partly as a joke and partly as a confession. The game hooked me because it met needs I didn't realize were unmet. It gave shape to our weeks, community to our town, and purpose to my work. Mostly, it reminded me of something simple: Joy can be disciplined. You can practice it, protect it, and build your life around it.

But here's the part I didn't understand until much later: Community isn't only something you build out there. The crowds, the travel, the tournaments, and the interviews were the visible forms of connection. They were important, meaningful, and alive. But they weren't the whole story. Even as my world expanded outward, something quieter was happening within. I was surrounded, supported, and deeply embedded in a community, but I hadn't yet learned how to bring that same presence home to the four walls where ordinary life happens.

There's a difference between being connected and being available for connection. I had mastered the first. The second was still catching up.

And that's where the next shift began, not under bright lights or on a livestream, but in the small, ordinary moments at home that asked me to slow down, put the phone down, look up, and actually be there. The next chapter isn't about cornhole at all. It's about learning how to let connection land in the quiet places, how to stop racing toward the next achievement long enough to notice the people right in front of me.

That's where everything changed next.

The Shift Home

By the time our cornhole world was at its busiest, with weekly tournaments, a growing club, livestreams, commentary, and travel, I was more connected than I had ever been. I had people everywhere. I had purpose, momentum, and a community that felt like family.

But connection isn't only measured by the number of people who know your name. It's measured by how fully you show up with the people who matter most. And that was the part I realized I'd been skimming. There were nights when the casino was buzzing, the cameras were rolling, and I could feel the electricity of belonging through every fist bump and every game. But when I walked through my own front door, a different kind of connection was waiting, one that didn't care about rankings, schedules, or who showed up in the livestream chat. Home is where relationships feel your pace. And mine had been fast for a very long time.

That's where the next season began. Not with more people, but with more presence. Not with more opportunities, but with more attention. The shift wasn't glamorous or public. It happened in small, unremarkable moments, the kind that are easy to miss when your brain is already halfway into tomorrow. This chapter is about those moments and what they taught me about belonging where it matters most.

There's a particular kind of drift that happens quietly, almost invisibly, when life becomes about keeping up. For years, I lived in a rhythm that appeared productive from the outside, running businesses, raising a family, checking boxes, and moving toward goals, but underneath was a feeling I couldn't quite name. It wasn't burnout. It wasn't depression. It was a distance. Distance from my own body. Distance from the people I loved. Distance from any moment that didn't feel useful or necessary.

What's confusing about this kind of drift is that it doesn't feel like numbness. It can feel like too much. I wasn't checked out, I was overly checked in. My nervous system was bracing, scanning, predicting. Every moment carried a low hum of urgency, as if I were running five minutes late to a life-or-death appointment I could never name. Nothing was wrong, yet everything felt like it might be if I stopped moving. My mind stayed three steps ahead of my body, planning the next task before the current one was halfway finished. I wasn't always disconnected from my feelings, but sometimes it felt as if I was drowning in them. And still, somehow, I wasn't actually in my life. It's hard to connect with other people when you're constantly trying to outrun a threat no one else can see.

My default setting has always been responsibility. I'm kind to myself, but I expect a lot. I move fast. I plan ahead. I take ownership of everything I touch. And when life gets full, the first thing I lose is presence. Not because I don't want to be present, but because my mind is always halfway into the next task. Even joy barely gets a full minute before the next thought pulls me forward.

It took me a long time to notice the cost of that pace. Even when my family was in the same room, I was often elsewhere, on my phone, answering messages, mentally working through a to-do list. Rome would come over and ask if I wanted to sit with him. Nick would call from the backyard. I wasn't avoiding them; I was just absorbed in a pattern of constant mental activity. But each time I chose the notification over the person, a thread loosened. Nothing broke, but connection thinned. And that thinning adds up.

After the fire and home invasion, I expected the trauma symptoms, the hypervigilance, the bracing, the difficulty relaxing. What I didn't expect was how disconnected I would feel inside my own home. Even long after we rebuilt our physical space, my internal sense of safety was shaky. My body was always a few steps ahead of my life, preparing for the next thing before the current one was even finished. For someone who had always relied on grit and momentum, slowing down wasn't intuitive. But the more I tried to fix it by working harder, the farther away connection felt.

What ultimately shifted things wasn't a plan, it was small interruptions. A question. An invitation. A doorway back into the moment.

There was an evening when the house felt scattered in that way families get when everyone is busy but no one is together. Nick stepped outside first. He didn't say anything at the time, but I could sense the invitation in the way he lingered by the door. Rome followed him instinctively. I stayed on the couch, phone in hand, scrolling through things I had already checked three times. It wasn't that I didn't want to join them. I just felt pulled by the momentum of my mind, finishing this, answering that, tying up the day.

But for some reason, something in me softened. I put my phone down and went outside.

Nothing dramatic happened. No big family moment. It was just the three of us sharing space. We threw a few bags, talked a little, and stood in silence a lot. Rome told a school story. Nick mentioned something he was building. I felt my shoulders drop without thinking about it. The air felt different. Not because of the game or the backyard or the evening light, but because my attention was finally where my feet were.

That moment taught me something I had never consciously understood: Connection doesn't require intensity. It requires availability. It doesn't need a perfectly planned family night. It just needs someone to say yes, right now, even if everything in your brain insists you should finish one more thing first.

Availability rarely looks dramatic. It looks like sitting down when your child pats the couch cushion. It looks like putting your phone face-down when a friend starts talking about something that matters. It looks like saying, "Sure, I'll come," even when the introverted part of you would rather stay home. Most of the connection we crave doesn't come from big gestures; it comes from small willingness.

I started noticing what changed in our home when I said yes more often. Conversations that would have been cut short stretched a little longer. Rome's stories got sillier and more detailed because he could tell I was actually listening. Nick didn't have to ask twice for me to come outside. He would just catch my eye, and I knew what he meant. Our house didn't get quieter; it got warmer. There was more laughter, more side hugs in hallways, more ordinary joy. These were the rewards – not achievements, not productivity – but presence.

It was quietly extraordinary to watch. While my professional world expanded, my life at home was teaching me that connection is a practice, not an achievement.

My son Rome doesn't want a perfect version of me. He wants the version that looks up when he asks for attention. My husband Nick doesn't need me to be endlessly productive. He needs me to join him in the yard without bringing my mental checklist along.

I've had to relearn this over and over, especially with my phone. What's interesting is that I've always had strong boundaries with technology when I'm out in the world. I don't take my phone out when I'm with friends. I don't scroll in restaurants or during conversations. I don't touch my phone in the car, ever. In public spaces, my attention stays with the people I'm with.

But at home, the rules slipped. Not intentionally, almost accidentally. My phone became a constant background presence. It was on the counter while I cooked, on the table while we watched TV, on the couch next to me while I rested. Any pause in the day, any moment of stillness, and I'd pick it up without thinking. I wasn't checking anything important. I wasn't even enjoying what I was looking at. It was just a reflex, a way of filling the smallest pockets of time.

That's what surprised me: I wasn't disconnected because

I didn't care. I was disconnected because my attention was leaking a dozen times an hour in ways that felt harmless. Notifications became tiny tugs. A quick check became a mental spiral. Entire evenings blurred, not because anything was wrong, but because I wasn't fully in the moments I cared about most.

Maybe you know that feeling, too.

You sit on the couch next to someone you love, but your mind is still online.

You pick up your phone just to check one thing, and 20 minutes evaporate.

You realize you've been in the same room but not really with the people in it.

It's not apathy. It's autopilot.

Do you ever feel your attention drift even when your heart wants to stay?

Do you find yourself refreshing apps you're not even interested in?

Do you catch yourself reaching for your phone before you realize why?

Most of us aren't choosing disconnection. It's choosing us, one tiny distraction at a time.

And we don't notice the loss until something important starts feeling far away.

The changes I made with my phone didn't come from theory. They came from necessity. I had to confront the reality that I couldn't feel connected when my attention was constantly fragmented. Presence isn't a personality trait. It's a choice we make moment to moment. And it's a choice made harder by the tools we carry everywhere.

But the flip side is powerful: Connection doesn't require massive changes. It requires interrupts. Small shifts. A willingness to stop mid-scroll when Rome asks to cuddle. A desire to step outside when Nick calls me. A willingness to show up to places where people gather, even when I'm tired, even when my mind tries to talk me out of it.

That is what this chapter is about: these small choices. The willingness to turn toward connection instead of away from it. To step into environments where belonging becomes more likely. To give your body enough presence to feel what your life actually holds. And to remember that connection doesn't come from grand moments. It comes from the tiny ones that ask almost nothing of you except that you show up.

This isn't the ending. It's the doorway to the next part of the book, a place where we move from stories and research into the practical ways connection can be lived, restored, and strengthened. But before we go there, it's worth pausing on this truth:

Connection doesn't ask you to be extraordinary. It asks you to be here.

And when you choose that, even for a moment, you'll find that everything you've been chasing feels closer, clearer, and more possible than ever.

Part III:

How Connection Actually Happens

Connection with Yourself: Why It Feels Hard to Be Here

Most people don't walk around saying, "I'm lonely" or "I need more connection." That's not the language we use. We say things like:

I'm exhausted.

I can't get motivated.

I feel stuck.

I don't know why I'm overwhelmed.

I can't focus.

I just want to feel like myself again.

We name the symptoms. We describe the surface-level frustration. We talk about our weight, our stress, our lack of discipline, our anxiety, our irritability, our inability to relax, our difficulty sleeping, our constant overthinking. We blame our schedule, our job, our partner, our hormones, our habits, our personality.

But underneath almost every one of those experiences sits a quieter truth we rarely name: We are disconnected, from ourselves, from others, or from a sense of meaning in our lives.

We say we want to be thinner, but we're usually longing for a body we feel safe and comfortable living in. We say we're overwhelmed, but often we're longing for support. When we feel unmotivated, it's usually not that we are lazy, but that we are depleted, unseen, or carrying more than others realize. When we say we "never have time", we're often living a life that leaves no space for breath, for presence, for being human. When we say we're anxious, we may not have a "thinking problem" but rather a not-safe-enough-to-connect problem.

And when we say we don't know what's wrong, it's almost always when we have been carrying too much alone for too long.

We rarely identify connection as the missing piece because disconnection doesn't feel like one big dramatic thing. It feels like tiny, everyday moments where we are physically present but emotionally elsewhere. It feels like nodding instead of feeling, surviving instead of participating, scrolling instead of speaking. Disconnection hides inside normal life. It masks itself as busyness, ambition, independence, or high standards. It looks productive. It feels familiar.

And modern life is built to amplify it.

You can see it anywhere people gather.

At red lights, phones light up before the car even stops moving.

In grocery lines, heads tilt down instead of up.

In waiting rooms, everyone is surrounded by people but interacting with none of them.

Even in our homes, the quiet moments that used to invite conversation, or at least awareness, now get filled with screens before we even notice our hands reaching for them.

It's not that we don't want connection.

It's that we've stopped leaving space for it.

Every pause becomes a check.

Every check becomes a habit.

Every habit becomes distance.

Connection requires openings: micro-moments where our attention softens and our bodies shift out of vigilance. But when our minds are constantly occupied, even by something as trivial as notifications or a running to-do list, those openings collapse. Not intentionally. Just gradually.

This is why connection feels so hard for so many people: We're not wired wrong. We're wired up too tightly. We're overstimulated, under-supported, emotionally saturated, and physically present but mentally elsewhere.

And we blame ourselves instead of the conditions.

We say we need to try harder.

We say we're bad at friendships.

We say we're introverted.

We say we're not "people people".

We say we're too busy, too awkward, too tired.

But the truth is simpler than the stories we tell ourselves. Connection requires safety, and most of us are too overstimulated or overextended to feel safe enough to soften.

Softening takes time.

Presence takes space.

Openness takes breath.

Belonging takes repetition.

And modern life is designed to eliminate all four.

This chapter isn't about blaming the world or blaming ourselves – or even about blaming phones. It's about finally naming what's underneath the struggle, not so we can shame ourselves into fixing it, but so we can stop fighting the wrong battles.

When you understand why connection feels hard, you stop interpreting it as a personal failing. You stop thinking something is wrong with you. You stop believing you're the only one struggling. You start seeing that the deepest longings in your life – ease, closeness, purpose, joy – aren't separate goals. They're all expressions of the same need.

The need to feel human again.

Once you begin to see connection as the root beneath so many of our struggles, something else becomes clear: Most of us learned to survive without it. Not because we didn't want closeness, but because closeness didn't always feel dependable. Maybe you grew up in a family system where you had to earn attention through performance or good behavior. Maybe you learned early that emotions made things harder, not easier. Maybe you had friendships that shifted without explanation, or partners who pulled away, or experiences that taught your nervous system to stay braced even in safe rooms.

These imprints don't disappear just because we become adults. They follow us quietly into our relationships, our work, our homes, and even our hobbies. They sit in the space between wanting connection and allowing it. They shape how we read silence, how we interpret closeness, how much vulnerability we'll risk.

People talk about attachment styles, trauma histories, and emotional wounds, but at the core, it's all the same story: Connection requires openness, and openness requires safety. If you've lived a life where safety was inconsistent, connection won't feel instinctive. It will feel earned. Managed. Negotiated. Something you have to be "good enough" for.

Even when there's no threat and no danger, your body doesn't know the difference between a friend who's genuinely busy and a childhood memory of being ignored. Your nervous system responds to patterns, not context. That's why connection feels risky even when it isn't. That's why closeness can feel overwhelming even when it's wanted. And that's why the people who seem the strongest, most capable, most reliable often struggle the most, because they've become experts at meeting everyone's needs except their own.

Connection becomes difficult when responsibility quietly turns into identity. When being reliable, productive, and capable becomes the primary way you secure your place in the world. Over time, your value starts to feel tied to what you produce or how well you manage everything around you. Slowing down feels irresponsible. Asking for help feels like asking too much. Rest starts to feel like a liability instead of a necessity.

So we respond the only way we know how. We decide we need to work on ourselves harder. Another routine. Another system. Another layer of discipline. We assume the solution is more control, less distraction, tighter management of our time and emotions. But connection doesn't thrive in control. It can't. Connection requires the opposite ... moments where you stop performing and allow yourself to simply exist.

The deeper truth is that most people don't struggle with connection itself. They struggle with the conditions connection requires. Connection needs unscheduled time and emotional availability. It needs attention that isn't constantly pulled away by a device. It needs a body that isn't living in a constant state of threat. It needs space for conversation, for silence, for nuance. It grows in moments when you're not rushing or bracing or analyzing or preparing. Moments when your nervous system is finally allowed to stand down. Very few adults ever get those conditions by accident. And even fewer protect them on purpose. We're not failing at connection. We're living in a world that leaves almost no room for it.

But once you see this, really see it, you understand why those rare moments of connection feel so healing. Why the simplest interactions can shift your entire nervous system. Why a conversation on a walk can feel better than a vacation. Why a shared laugh can feel like oxygen. Why certain environments make you feel alive while others make you shut down.

Your body knows when connection is possible. It also knows when it isn't.

Which is why, when people ask me how cornhole changed my life, I never talk about the game first. I talk about the *conditions*. The rhythm. The predictability. The shared focus. The side-by-side posture instead of face-to-face intensity. The sense of equality. The lack of pretense. The space between throws. The repetition of seeing the same faces week after week until nervousness turned into familiarity, and familiarity turned into belonging.

It wasn't the game itself. It was the structure. The container. The doorway.

But that doorway could have been anything, any space where people gather with enough consistency, enough openness, enough rhythm for connection to become possible.

Cornhole just happened to be the one that found me when I needed it most.

And once I began to understand this, something clicked: Connection is not an outcome. It's an environment. It's not something you do. It's something you allow. And for most of us, allowing connection requires unlearning years of bracing, rushing, performing, and distracting ourselves out of the present moment.

The rest of this chapter is about what that unlearning looks like in real life. Not from a clinical perspective, but from the inside, from the small, human ways connection begins to return once you start creating even a little bit of space for it.

Because most of us are far closer to connection than we realize.

We're usually one breath away.

One pause away.

One softened moment away.

One opened posture away.

One "yes" away.

Connection doesn't require perfect timing. It requires permission.

And when we start giving ourselves that permission, even in tiny doses, we stop living at the edge of our lives and start living inside them again.

Unlearning also requires honesty about the environment we're living in. Not judgment. Not shame. Just clarity.

I've already shared I once believed I had strong tech boundaries, and in certain parts of life, I truly did. But at home, every pause became a check and every check became a habit. I don't need to retell that here. What matters now is this: The frantic way most of us live isn't a personal flaw. It's the world we're trying to survive.

The problem isn't the phone. The problem is what it replaces.

For generations, the quiet pauses in our day, the walk to the mailbox, the space between tasks, the moment before the water boils, were where we came back to ourselves. Those were the slivers where we noticed our own thoughts, felt our emotions, or just existed in our bodies. Those in-between spaces were the original doorway to self-connection.

Now those spaces are gone.

Our nervous system wasn't built for constant stimulation or constant comparison. It was built for attunement. For pacing. For presence. We haven't lost connection because we're careless. We've lost it because modern life leaves almost no room for the things that make us human.

And this is where the deeper unlearning begins: We must remember what being human actually requires.

To be human is to be heard — and that starts internally. Most of us don't listen to our own cues until they're screaming. We override hunger, exhaustion, intuition, and discomfort. Hearing ourselves means noticing the quiet signals before they turn into symptoms.

Practical shift: Ask yourself once a day, "What is my body saying right now?" Not what you *should* feel. What you *do* feel.

To be human is to be uplifted — not by validation from others, but by the way you speak to yourself. Most high achievers don't need more confidence; they need a break from the voice that treats them like a problem to solve.

Practical shift: Replace self-critique with a simple acknowledgment: "That was a lot today. I handled it." You don't need cheerleading. You need accurate kindness.

To be human is to feel meaningful — not because of what you produce, but because your inner world matters. We live in a culture that measures worth by output. When your value is tied to productivity, rest feels like failure, and stillness feels unsafe.

Practical shift: Do one thing each day that has meaning but no measurable outcome. Sit outside, doodle, stretch, breathe. Let something matter simply because it matters to you.

To be human is to have autonomy — the ability to choose rather than react. Rigid rules and black-and-white thinking slowly take that away. When everything feels non-negotiable, you stop experiencing your life as a series of choices and start experiencing it as a list of demands. Pace replaces agency. Should replaces desire. You move through the day reacting instead of deciding.

Practical shift: Create one moment of choice each day. Pause before responding. Decide when you'll check your phone instead of checking it automatically. Ask yourself how you want the next hour to feel, and let that answer guide you.

And to be human is to feel nurtured — supported, steady, and safe within yourself. Nurture is the condition that allows everything else to work. Your nervous system can't connect to others if it doesn't feel cared for internally.

Practical shift: Pick one nurturing behavior and make it predictable: going to bed on time, a nightly walk, a boundary around screen use, or a few minutes of stillness before sleep. Reliability creates safety.

These five experiences: hearing yourself, uplifting yourself, feeling meaningful, choosing intentionally, and nurturing your inner world, are the basic ingredients of being human.

When you look closely, you'll notice something important:

Every single one of these requires space. Not hours. Not a retreat. Just moments where nothing is competing for your attention.

Which is why unlearning disconnection isn't about perfection or discipline; it's about reclaiming the gaps modern life has stolen. Because when you give yourself even a little breathing room, something surprising happens: Your humanity rushes back in.

And that's the foundation for every connection that comes next.

Once you can hear yourself, uplift yourself, feel meaningful within yourself, choose for yourself, and nurture yourself, you stop searching for other people to fill those gaps.

You begin to show up with others from a place of wholeness, not hunger.

That's where the next chapter begins.

Connection with Others: Presence, Attention, and Choosing People over Pace

I used to judge people quickly. Faster than I ever admitted out loud. Someone would complain too much, move too slow, interrupt a conversation, show up late, or make a choice I didn't understand, and my mind would leap to the simplest explanation: They should try harder. They should know better. They should get it together. It felt efficient at the time, clean, quick, tidy. Except it wasn't true.

When I started working with people on their health and weight years ago, this pattern became impossible to ignore. I'd mention a client – a woman who had gained weight steadily over the past year, a man struggling with late-night binge eating, a girl who couldn't stay consistent with exercise – and instantly people filled in the blanks with assumptions. "Oh, so they need to eat less and move more." "They probably just love fast food." "They're being lazy."

But if I had shared the *real* reasons – unbearable grief, an abusive marriage, bankruptcy, childhood trauma, caregiving responsibilities, depression, a loneliness so deep they didn't know how to speak it – those same people would have been devastated for them. Not judging. Not dismissive. Heartbroken.

That helped it click for me: You can only judge people when you're disconnected from them. Judgment requires distance. Assumptions require not knowing. The closer you move toward someone's story, the quieter the judgment becomes.

It changed my lens of the world. The coworker who seemed rude? May be caring for a mother with cancer. The friend who became distant? May be drowning under financial pressure they haven't named. The neighbor who never waves back? May be grieving someone they loved. The stranger who snaps? May be carrying more than anyone can see.

Unfortunately, most of us don't want to know all these reasons. Not because we're unkind or uncaring, but because we're overloaded. We feel we can't take on one more thing. It feels easier to flatten people into characters than to be human with them. It feels easier to tell a story that protects our distance than to allow a story that pulls us closer.

But every time we choose that version, something in us disconnects, too.

The more I paid attention, the more I realized how easy it has become to live in a world of half-stories. We see the behavior, not the human. We react to the surface and move on. And because life moves fast, because we're tired, because our attention is scattered across 100 tiny demands, we rarely slow down long enough to ask ourselves the one question that changes everything: What might be going on for them?

It didn't used to be like this. Connection used to be woven into the fabric of daily life. Neighbors talked on front porches.

People sat on stoops or at kitchen tables and told stories without rushing. Children played in the street while adults lingered in the shared edges of their days. There were pauses built into the rhythm of life, natural pockets where you'd run into people, where someone would ask how you were and actually stay long enough to hear the answer. We didn't have to fight for connection. It was the default.

The default now is distance. Not because people are worse, but because our world is louder. Faster. More fragmented. We rush from thing to thing. We communicate in shortcuts. We assume before we ask. We scroll through curated versions of each other's lives and forget there's always a fuller picture. Even in groups, we often stay parallel, close enough to appear connected, far enough that nothing vulnerable has to be risked. The result is subtle but profound: We begin relating to people as roles rather than humans. The barista. The coworker. The parent in the car line. The person blocking the aisle. The partner who didn't say what we needed them to say. The friend who didn't respond fast enough.

When we reduce people to their function in our day, empathy disappears. Curiosity disappears. Generosity disappears. And connection doesn't just become harder, it becomes impossible.

But here's the hopeful part: The moment we remember that every person carries an unseen story, something softens. The sharpness eases. The urgency fades. The space between us becomes a little less defended.

That's the doorway to connection. And it begins long before we ever open our mouths. It begins with the way we see people. It begins with remembering what makes us human in the first place.

For me, this understanding didn't arrive in a single moment; it unfolded slowly, through thousands of encounters in gyms, backyards, workplaces, airports, tournaments, and living rooms. Again and again, I saw that people are starving to feel human with each other. They want to feel heard. They want to feel acknowledged. They want to feel like their presence matters. They want to feel free to be themselves. And they want to feel cared for in small, ordinary ways that don't require performance.

Those desires aren't random. They're universal. They're ancient. They're wired into us.

Without naming the framework or turning this into a lesson, I started to see the pattern. Connection grows when people feel heard. When they feel uplifted. When they feel meaningful. When they feel autonomous, free to be themselves instead of who someone else prefers. And when they feel nurtured and met with steadiness instead of sharpness, warmth instead of dismissal.

The reverse is also true.

Disconnection grows when people feel ignored.

When they feel criticized.

When they feel invisible.

When they feel controlled.

When they feel unsafe.

No relationship is immune to this – not romantic ones, not friendships, not coworkers, not families. Even the healthiest groups can drift into patterns of rushing, misunderstanding, or assuming the worst. Not because anyone intends harm, but because connection takes attention. It takes noticing. It takes remembering to be human with each other in a world that constantly pushes us toward speed and reaction.

I've watched this happen in workplaces where employees sit 10 feet from each other but feel miles apart. In families where everyone loves each other deeply but keeps missing one another emotionally. In friend groups where no one wants to burden anyone else, so everyone carries more than they should in silence. In communities where one conflict, one miscommunication, one misunderstood tone fractures everything because no one slowed down long enough to ask, "What's the story behind this?"

The truth is, connection isn't complicated. It's just inconvenient.

It asks us to pause.

To consider.

To open.

To stay curious a moment longer than we stay defensive.

Once I started paying attention, I realized that increasing connection with others isn't complicated. It's not about becoming more social or extroverted or charismatic. It's about practicing a few deeply human behaviors in ordinary moments. Most of them take under 10 seconds. Most of them cost nothing. But they change everything.

The first is hearing people, not just their words, but what their words are protecting. Most of us talk in hints. A coworker says, "I'm just tired," but the pause afterward tells you it's more than that. A friend jokes about being overwhelmed, but their eyes flick away before they add more. People rarely hand us the full truth of their experience; they offer a corner of it and wait to see if we'll care enough to notice. Being human with people means noticing. It means listening for the sentence beneath the sentence. It means responding in a way that says, "I'm here. You're not invisible." You don't need perfect responses. Presence counts more than precision.

The second is uplift. Not flattery or performance, just small acknowledgments that remind people they matter. I've seen rooms transformed by a simple "I'm glad you made it." A parent softens when you say, "I know you're doing your best." A coworker straightens a little when you mention you noticed their effort. Encouragement doesn't need to be dramatic. In fact, the quieter it is, the more powerful it often feels. People are starved for real noticing. Noticing reconnects people to themselves, and in doing so, reconnects them to each other.

Connection also deepens when people feel meaningful. Not useful or impressive but meaningful. When their presence, not their productivity, shifts something. The friend who brings calm into a room without saying much; the coworker who remembers birthdays; the neighbor who always waves. People need the sense that who they are, not just what they do, contributes to the emotional temperature around them. When you name those contributions in others, even subtly, they show up more fully. And when you notice them in yourself, you stop chasing worthiness and start embodying it.

Autonomy matters, too. People can't connect when they feel controlled, judged, or managed. One of the fastest ways to build trust is to give people space to be themselves. To let them move at their own pace, share on their own timeline, and opt in rather than being pulled. I've learned this the hard way in friendships and family. When someone felt me trying to "fix" them, they withdrew. When I stepped back and offered choice, "Want to talk or just sit together?" "Want advice or just company?" the connection deepened instantly. People move closer when they feel free.

And then there's nurture, the tone beneath everything. Nurture isn't coddling or overprotecting. It's about creating emotional softness around the people you care about. It's checking in without pressure. It's asking how someone is and actually waiting long enough to hear the answer. It's offering calm when someone else is carrying chaos. It's saying, "I've got you," in whatever form your relationship holds. When nurture is present, people settle. When nurture is absent, people brace.

These five needs – being heard, being uplifted, feeling meaningful, being autonomous, and feeling nurtured – aren't just abstract ideas. They are the emotional physics of connection. They govern how safe people feel, how open they become, and how deeply they bond. Once you start using them as a lens, everything sharpens. You see why a conversation lands wrong. You see why someone pulls away. You see why a room feels tense or a relationship feels off. Disconnection is rarely personal. It's almost always one of these five needs going unmet.

What makes this even more powerful is how simple the shifts can be. You don't need scripts or social techniques. You need micro-moments of humanity. A soft tone where there used to be impatience. Curiosity where there used to be assumption. A pause where there used to be reaction. A smile where there used to be distraction. And the more you practice these tiny shifts, the more natural they become.

I've seen friendships revive from a single honest conversation. I've seen strained marriages soften because one partner stopped defending and started listening. I've seen workplaces transform when leaders gave people more autonomy and more acknowledgment. None of these changes required dramatic interventions. They required consistent, gentle humanity.

Connection grows wherever people feel safe enough to show up. And safety grows wherever humanity is practiced. That's the heart of it.

Connection in Community – the Places Belonging Takes Shape

Community sounds like something that just exists somewhere, something you join, something you find, something a lucky few have without trying. But real community isn't something you stumble into. It's something that forms through thousands of tiny moments of humanity layered over time. And the truth is, most people don't realize how much community they're missing until they finally experience it again.

For most of human history, community wasn't a choice; it was the condition in which we lived. People didn't need to "schedule quality time". They bumped into each other at wells, markets, front porches, sidewalks. Kids played in the street together because there was nothing else to do. Neighbors borrowed sugar because the store wasn't open late. Elders sat on porches and waved at anyone who walked by. Life wasn't always quieter, but it was closer. Daily life nudged you into connection.

Modern life, for all its progress, redesigned the world in a way that quietly stripped us of the places where connection used to happen without effort. Houses are bigger, farther apart, and designed for privacy. Neighborhoods prioritize cars instead of feet. Commutes eat daylight. Coffee shops are filled with headphones, not conversations. The places we used to gather – churches, PTA meetings, neighborhood potlucks, front lawns – now compete with schedules that leave almost no extra margin. The moment our days became full, our communities became empty.

And then came phones, designed to meet our social instincts just enough to keep us from noticing how socially starved we've become. We scroll through people we know without ever speaking to them. We "like" posts instead of knocking on a door. We comment instead of calling. We watch other people's lives instead of participating in our own. The illusion of connection has replaced the experience of it.

This isn't a moral failing. It's a structural one. We're living in a world where the natural friction that used to create community has been replaced by convenience. We don't have to rely on neighbors anymore. We don't have to show up anywhere. We don't have to work through tension with people we'll see again tomorrow. We can choose comfort over connection every single time, and no one will call us on it. Modern life gives us more options but fewer anchors.

When community disappears, something inside us goes quiet. We stop being known. We stop being mirrored. We stop being shaped by the soft edges of everyday interactions. The nervous system loses those micro-reminders of safety. The heart loses the steady beat of belonging. Even people surrounded by coworkers, acquaintances, or online friends can feel a hollowness they can't quite name.

Humans, when disconnected from community, do what humans always do: We start imagining each other instead of knowing each other. We fill in the blanks with assumptions. We see inconvenience as rudeness. We see difference as threat. We see strangers as obstacles instead of potential allies. When we don't have proximity, we lose context. And without context, we dehumanize each other without even realizing we're doing it.

Most people don't walk around saying, "I need more community." We tell ourselves we're fine because we have a couple close friends, or a partner, or a family group chat. When you're a kid or a teenager, you don't have to think about community at all; it's built into your days. School hallways, sports teams, lunch tables, after-school hangouts. You have proximity, repetition, shared experiences, and the constant presence of peers. You don't join community; you're immersed in it.

But adulthood rearranges all of that. Suddenly your world shrinks to the places you have to be: work, home, errands, kids' activities. The spontaneous, low-stakes environments where connection used to grow, the spaces sociologists call "third places", quietly disappear. A third place is any environment that isn't home and isn't work, where you can show up, be known without being evaluated, and participate without pressure. It's the thing that keeps a person rooted in their town, not just residing in it.

For most people, those places simply don't exist anymore. We convince ourselves we don't need them. We tell ourselves we're too introverted, too tired, too busy. We assume deep friendship is the same thing as community. But close friends and a community serve different emotional functions. Your close friends are where you go for support. Community is where you go to feel alive. One keeps you grounded; the other expands you. One reminds you who you are; the other reminds you you're part of something bigger.

When we lose community, most people don't even realize it's missing. They just feel duller. Heavier. Less hopeful. Life starts to feel like a loop instead of a landscape. You stop meeting new people. You stop having new conversations. You stop hearing fresh ideas. You stop being influenced by perspectives outside your home or workplace. Your world becomes small.

What makes this especially tricky is that nothing is "wrong". You can love your family, love your friends, love your job, and still feel a quiet ache you can't fully name. That ache is a lack of place. It's the absence of a setting where you can be a participant in something larger than your personal life.

A true community pushes you in ways your inner circle can't. It introduces you to people you wouldn't normally choose. It exposes you to different personalities, different stories, different ways of being human. It gives you the experience of belonging with people who don't share your DNA or your history or your daily routines. And that kind of belonging expands your sense of self. It stretches your edges. It strengthens the psychological muscles that connection depends on, such as listening, patience, empathy, adaptability, and social trust.

Community also adds something no small friend group can replicate: visibility without pressure. Being recognized without being responsible for anyone. Being welcomed without having to perform. Being part of the room without being the center of it. For people who carry a lot of responsibility, such as parents, caretakers, leaders, and high performers, this kind of belonging is restorative in a way intimacy alone cannot provide.

This is why relying solely on family or a couple friends leaves a gap. Not because those relationships aren't enough, but because they serve a different purpose. Humans need both depth and breadth. We need roots and horizon. We need people who know us intimately, and people who simply know our name and light up when we walk through the door.

Without community, life becomes something you manage. With community, life becomes something you participate in.

What I kept noticing, the more I paid attention, was how community doesn't rise or fall on big gestures. It rises or falls on the emotional tone people bring into a room. The difference between a place that feels alive and a place that feels flat is almost always the difference between people who show up guarded and people who show up willing.

And that willingness can be felt.

I've watched the atmosphere lift, like someone cracked a window and let oxygen in. One person arrives open enough to listen, warm enough to greet someone first, steady enough to not take things personally, curious enough to ask a real question, relaxed enough to laugh, and suddenly the entire room shifts around them. People mirror it without even thinking about it.

Community grows through emotional modeling. Healthy communities need at least one person in the room who is quietly practicing what it means to be human. Not performing it. Not intellectualizing it. Living it. Someone who listens a little more fully than expected. Someone who offers warmth before knowing whether it will be returned. Someone who extends patience when irritation would be easier. Someone who makes room for mistakes, personalities, and differences. Someone who carries a posture soft enough that other people relax the moment they enter the space.

The opposite was just as true. Anytime even one of those elements was missing, the room contracted. I've been in groups where everyone was polite but no one was truly listening, and the entire space felt hollow. I've been in meetings where competence mattered more than care, and the energy sharpened until people shut down. I've been in environments where people clung tightly to their way of doing things, and newcomers felt like intruders instead of additions. I've also been in spaces that were busy, loud, and full of people, yet emotionally barren.

These revelations came before my theory of HUMAN™ was even a framework for understanding connection. It was something I saw in the wild long before I had language for it — a reminder of how to be human again with ourselves, our bodies, and each other in a world that makes it easy to forget. People felt heard because someone bothered to notice. They felt uplifted because someone acknowledged their effort. They felt meaningful because their presence subtly changed the room. They felt autonomous because no one tried to force them into a mold. And they felt nurtured because the atmosphere was warm enough to breathe in. When those five things were present, community didn't need to be engineered.

It emerged naturally.

What actually breaks communities isn't conflict. It's disconnection. And disconnection is almost always the absence of one of those very human needs. The good news is that repairing it rarely requires sweeping change. More often, it begins with the smallest, most ordinary acts: a genuine hello, a moment of eye contact, remembering someone's name, sharing a little more of yourself than is strictly necessary. It shows up when you let someone else go first, allow difference without correction, and make room for pauses instead of rushing to fill them. It's asking a real question instead of a throwaway one, or telling someone, "I'm glad you made it," even if they only came once. These are the behaviors that give a community its pulse.

I've watched people who thought they were "bad with others" become the emotional center of a group simply by practicing these tiny acts of humanity. I've watched introverts quietly become anchors because they listened deeply. I've watched the shyest people create connection simply by being steady. You don't need charisma to build community, you just need presence.

And here's the surprising part: When you offer humanity to others, it returns to you twice as strong. The more you listen, the more listened-to you feel. The more warmth you extend, the more warmth you receive. The more meaningful you make others feel, the more meaningful your place becomes. The more freedom you give people to be themselves, the safer you feel being yourself. The more nurture you offer, the more held you feel. As a result, connection isn't something we teach to other people; it's something we practice until it becomes the atmosphere around us.

The moment you start bringing that into the spaces you're part of, whether it's a workplace, gym, friend group, school, club, or neighborhood, the whole place recalibrates. Not immediately. Not dramatically. But steadily. Predictably. Almost quietly.

Communities don't change when the group shifts. Communities change when the tone shifts. And the tone shifts when even one person decides to show up with a little more humanity than they did the day before.

That's the real work of connection in community.

Not grand plans. Not flawless systems.

Humanity, practiced in small, steady ways.

If there's one thing I hope you take from this book, it's this: You don't have to overhaul your life to build connection. You don't need more confidence, more charisma, or more time. You just need more humanity, your own. A little more listening, a little more noticing, a little more willingness to show up even when you're tired or unsure. Those small choices create the conditions where community can take root. And once it does, everything changes. We feel safer. Braver. Softer. More ourselves. The world gets easier to live in. Connection isn't a destination; it's a rhythm, one you can step into anytime you choose.

In Closing

The night of the fire is still etched in my memory. The glow on the ridge, the frantic escape, the strange silence afterward when everything familiar was gone. In the months that followed, survival was the only focus: food, clothes, somewhere to sleep. But what I missed most wasn't the things. It was belonging. Home had never been about four walls. It was people, routine, community, and laughter. The fire stripped that from me.

Months later, in a local cornhole tournament, I saw a glimpse of what had been lost. A few boards and bags, neighbors gathered to throw. It wasn't polished, but it was enough. That night whispered to me, "You can rebuild. You can belong."

I didn't know it then, but that moment was the beginning of everything you've just read. It led me from ashes to connection, from rebuilding to play, from isolation to community. Along the way, I learned our culture makes disconnection incredibly easy, while connection is something we can choose with intention, through presence, attention, and the courage to be seen.

The HUMAN™ framework at the end of this book details what life, research, and community taught me, that we thrive when we are heard, uplifted, meaningful, autonomous, and nurtured. When those needs are met, motivation rises naturally. When they're ignored, even success feels hollow. HUMAN™ isn't a tool for self-improvement; it's a way of remembering.

Cornhole happened to be what reintroduced me to my inner need for connection. It turned neighbors into friends, players into family, and strangers into a community that holds me. Through that simple game, I've traveled the country, met thousands of people, and watched connection heal more than competition ever could. People often think my career evolved because I chased opportunities. It didn't. Most doors opened because I was physically present in spaces where connection could happen. I showed up to tournaments not because I saw a pathway forward, but because I felt drawn to the energy of people being together.

But the deeper lesson wasn't about the game, it was about what happens when people gather with openness, consistency, and no agenda other than being together. Everything that's followed, the podcast, cornhole courses, the retreats, and even the reality series, grew from that foundation. I didn't build them through hustling harder. I built them by choosing connection over performance, presence over productivity, and community over isolation. When I live HUMAN™, when I listen, celebrate, find meaning, choose freely, and nurture gently, opportunity expands without force.

If the fire was the ending of one story, this is the beginning of another. Connection rebuilt what loss destroyed. It reminded me that no matter how uncertain the future looks, belonging is always within reach. All it takes is a single step, a softened moment, a small yes, an open posture.

But knowing that connection matters isn't the same as living it.

We live in a world that pulls us away from ourselves, from our bodies, from each other. Remembering how to be human doesn't happen by accident. It happens through small, intentional shifts practiced over time.

So before we close this book, I want to give you something tangible. Not theory. Not inspiration. Practice.

In the next section, I'll walk you through the simple tools that helped me come home to myself and the people around me: The Unplugged framework, the HUMAN diagnostic, and the unexpected doorway of play that made connection real in my everyday life.

Because connection doesn't wait for perfect timing. It begins wherever you are, with whatever you have, and it grows one human moment at a time.

Part IV:

Align, Play, Grow

A Guide to Being Unplugged AF (Aligned & Focused)

RULE 1 — No Phone First Thing in the Morning

For the first moments of your day, your phone stays untouched. Let your body wake you up, not everyone else's thoughts, needs, or notifications. This is where presence begins.

RULE 2 — No Phone before Bed

For the last 30 minutes of your night, your phone is done for the day. Your brain needs the signal that you're winding down, not revving up. This alone improves sleep, anxiety, and mental clarity.

RULE 3 — No Phones in Motion

If your body is moving, your phone is parked. Walking, pacing, going room to room, no checking. Stops the autopilot grab-and-scroll reflex.

RULE 4 — No Phones during Micro-Moments

These are the moments that used to create connection and calm:

- Red lights
- Waiting in line
- Waiting for water to boil
- Waiting to pick up kids
- Sitting down between tasks

These stay phone-free.

RULE 5 — Phone in Its Home (and Notifications Off)

Choose one spot in your house – a counter, a shelf, or a basket – and that's where your phone lives when you're home. Keep the ringer on, but turn off all notifications except calls and texts. Notifications are micro-distractions. Even when you don't check them, your brain does. A buzz, a banner, a vibration, a preview, it all creates tiny pulls that keep you half in, half out of your life. With notifications off, your phone stops acting like a tug on your attention. With a home base, it stops following you from room to room. You go to it intentionally.

RULE 6 — No Phone during Human Moments

If someone is talking to you, next to you, hugging you, or asking for attention: phone goes down. Face-to-face wins, always.

RULE 7 — Intentional Scroll Windows

Pick intentional times for catching up, scrolling, responding, and checking. Outside that window, you use your phone with intention, not impulse.

A Guide to Cornhole

Most people who consider trying cornhole are either curious or nervous. Sometimes both.

Maybe you've seen a tournament on TV. Maybe you've watched people playing at a park or brewery. Maybe someone invited you to a local event, and your first thought was, I'll embarrass myself.

If that's you, you're not alone.

Almost everyone walks into their first night feeling unsure about their skill, their social confidence, or whether they "belong" in a room full of people who seem to know what they're doing. This chapter is here to bridge that gap, to help you take a simple step toward something that can change your life far more than you expect.

Cornhole is not about being good. It's not about winning. It's not about gear or strategy or perfect technique. It's about belonging, and belonging starts with showing up.

This chapter will walk you through the basics so you can feel confident enough to walk into your first throw, your first game, or your first local event, even if you've never held a beanbag.

Why Cornhole Works (Even If You've Never Played Anything Before)

Cornhole is one of the easiest games for beginners.

You don't need training.

You don't need experience.

You don't need athleticism.

You don't even need coordination, as you'll develop that as you go.

But more importantly, cornhole has a unique structure that makes connection almost inevitable.

Two boards, a few bags, and a steady rhythm: throw, pause, throw, pause.

Those pauses are where conversation happens naturally.

The atmosphere is competitive enough to be engaging, but relaxed enough that no one takes themselves too seriously.

Most people walk in strangers and walk out with someone they talked to, laughed with, or learned from.

Skill comes later.

Belonging comes first.

What You Need to Get Started

1. Boards: Regulation boards are 27 feet apart for competitive play — but beginners can move them closer. You can use any backyard boards, folding boards, borrowed boards, or boards set up at local events.
2. Bags: You can start with basic fabric bags. If you want to upgrade later, you can — but it's not necessary. Most local

events have loaner bags so you don't have to buy anything at all.

3. Space: A yard, a driveway, a park, or anywhere with flat ground works. If you don't have access to boards at home, almost every city has weekly public tournaments or open play nights where you can try before investing.

4. A Willingness to Show Up: This is the hardest part for most people. Everything else is optional.

How to Throw (The Simple Version)

There are countless techniques, but to begin, you only need one idea:

- Hold the bag like you're shaking someone's hand.
- Swing your arm straight.
- Release the bag about shoulder height with the palm up.
- Your only job is to make a flat throw, everything else is bonus.

Most beginners improve dramatically in the first 20 minutes. You don't need to master anything before your first event.

What to Expect at a Local Event

This is where most people feel intimidated, so let's demystify it. You'll walk in and see lanes of boards, people chatting, and a pretty relaxed vibe. Some attendees take the game seriously, but most are just happy to be there.

You'll be welcomed. Local tournament directors are used to first-timers and go out of their way to help.

Your partner might be a stranger. Most events use random pairings, which means you won't need to bring a partner.

You'll meet someone new within the first five minutes.

People will encourage you. Cornhole culture is almost shockingly supportive. Someone will say, "Nice bag!" Someone will fist-bump you. Someone will tell you they just started, too.

You don't need to know how to keep score. Someone else will help. You'll learn immediately by doing.

One night is enough to know if this is your community. Most people feel it within a single game.

How to Find a Club or Weekly Tournament

I've put together a simple directory and guidance to help you locate local weekly tournaments, "switch" or "swap" meets, beginner-friendly nights, free open-play options, and social clubs, bars, or breweries that host casual games. You can start as soon as this week.

How to Show Up When You Feel Nervous

Everyone feels this way the first time. Use these practices:

1. Go with curiosity, not confidence. You're not expected to know anything.
2. Tell the director you're new, and you'll be looked out for all night.
3. Focus on people, not performance. You're not there to win. You're there to be in a room where connection is easy.
4. Celebrate effort, not outcomes. Every bag you throw is progress. Every conversation is connection. Every night you show up rewires something in your nervous system.
5. Remember: Most people in that room don't care how you play. They care that you came. If you encounter an occasional

overly competitive person, ignore them. The vast majority are thrilled a new person has found the game. A couple serious players should never ruin your chance at finding something that can bring you joy.

What Will Happen if You Stick with It

You'll get better at the game, yes. But the deeper changes are the ones you'll feel in your life:

- You'll have somewhere consistent to go every week.
- You'll have people who notice when you walk in.
- You'll laugh more often.
- You'll feel more grounded.
- Your body will relax in ways your mind can't force.
- You'll start to belong, not because you earned it, but because you showed up.

Cornhole is one of the simplest, most accessible ways to rebuild community, connection, and joy. You never know who you'll meet, what opportunities will open, or how much lighter life can feel. The only way to find out is to take the first step.

When you're ready to start, I built a page with everything you need: CornholeMeesh.com/start.

It's your doorway into a world you may not know exists yet – one bag, one night, one connection at a time.

A Quick Primer to the HUMAN™ Framework

There may be moments as you finish this book when something feels off, and you don't immediately know why. You might feel irritable, unmotivated, disconnected, restless, or even numb. You might feel like you should be fine, but you aren't. If this happens, the goal isn't to fix yourself. It's to listen to an awareness that is making itself known for the first time in a long time: You crave connection.

The good news is this signal opens the door to change. The HUMAN™ framework I've created is a way to orient, or perhaps, reorient. It's a way to ask better questions when your system is signaling that something essential is missing.

When things feel off, pause and ask yourself which of these needs might be unmet right now. Often, one of these needs will stand out immediately.

H — Heard

Ask yourself: *Do I feel heard — by someone else, or by myself?*

Disconnection often shows up here as frustration,

defensiveness, or the urge to overexplain. Sometimes it means you need to speak something out loud. Other times, it means you've been rushing past your own internal signals. A small repair might look like naming what you're feeling without justifying it, writing one honest sentence, or telling someone, "I don't need advice, I just need to say this."

U — Uplifted

Ask yourself: *When was the last time I felt encouraged, appreciated, or acknowledged?*

When uplift is missing, the inner voice often turns harsh or transactional. You might notice yourself minimizing wins or moving immediately to the next task.

A repair doesn't require hype. It can be as simple as letting something go well and allowing yourself to register it. Or offering one genuine sentence of encouragement to yourself or someone else and letting it land.

M — Meaningful

Ask yourself: *Does what I'm doing right now feel connected to something that matters to me?*

When meaning is absent, life can feel flat even if you're busy. You may feel bored, resentful, or strangely empty despite being productive.

A repair might be reconnecting a task to its purpose, changing how you're doing it, or choosing one small action that aligns with your values instead of your obligations.

A — Autonomous

Ask yourself: *Do I feel like I'm choosing this, or obeying a rule?*

When autonomy is missing, life becomes rigid. You tell yourself there's a right way and a wrong way. Flexibility disappears, and choice gets replaced by pressure. Even well-intentioned habits start to feel heavy when they're driven by obligation instead of agency.

Repairing autonomy doesn't mean abandoning structure. It means reintroducing choice. A cookie can be nourishing when it's eaten with presence instead of shame. Rest can be restorative. Stretching is movement. Autonomy returns when you allow yourself to ask, What would feel supportive right now? and trust the answer without immediately overriding it.

N — Nurtured

Ask yourself: *Is my body supported right now?*

When nurture is lacking, you may feel exhausted, wired, disconnected from your body, or unable to settle.

A repair might be physical before it's emotional. This could mean water, movement, rest, warmth, stepping outside, or simply slowing your breathing enough for your nervous system to register safety.

You don't need to meet every need all the time. Being human means needs fluctuate. What matters is recognizing them before you override them with discipline, distraction, or self-criticism.

If you're using HUMAN™ in a moment of tension with someone else, you can also gently ask: Which of these needs might be unmet here, for me or for them? That single shift often softens the story you're telling and opens space for connection instead of conflict.

HUMAN™ is a way to notice what's missing without making yourself wrong. When you start responding to needs instead of fighting symptoms, connection with yourself and others becomes less effortful and more natural. It's not about becoming more disciplined. It's about remembering how to be human, and letting that be enough.

about

DR. MICHELLE HASTIE THOMPSON

Dr. Michelle Hastie Thompson is a researcher, speaker, and creator of the HUMAN™ framework, a model that helps people understand why connection is essential for well-being, confidence, and sustainable performance. Known to many as Cornhole Meesh, she works at the intersection of psychology, play, and human connection, helping individuals and organizations reconnect to what makes them feel grounded, alive, and supported.

She commentates professional cornhole, creates courses, leads coaching experiences, and designs team-based connection events that use play and shared experience to build trust, presence, and belonging. Her work focuses on practical, human ways to restore focus, emotional regulation, and resilience in a world that often pulls people away from themselves and each other.

Michelle lives in California with her husband, Nick, and their son, Rome, where most of her best ideas still begin in the backyard, one throw at a time.

also by

DR. MICHELLE HASTIE THOMPSON

Absolute Love Publishing is an independent book publisher devoted to creating and publishing books that promote goodness in the world.

www.absolutelovepublishing.com

www.ingramcontent.com/pod-product-compliance
Lightning Source LLC
LaVergne TN
LVHW010627100826
845148LV00014B/3140

* 9 7 9 8 9 8 5 5 7 4 6 5 4 *